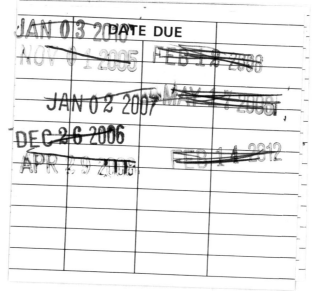

Korean Holidays
&
Festivals

Also by Frances M. Koh

English-Korean Picture Dictionary

Creative Korean Cooking

Oriental Children in American Homes

Korean Holidays

&
Festivals

By Frances M. Koh

Illustrations by Liz B. Dodson

EastWest Press
Minneapolis • Minnesota

*Special thanks to Sul-Hee Kim, who aided in research
and provided updated information for this book.*

Library of Congress Catalog Card Number: 90-84031
International Standard Book Number: 0-9606090-5-9

First Edition

Design by Frances M. Koh
Printed in the United States of America

To Children Everywhere

CONTENTS

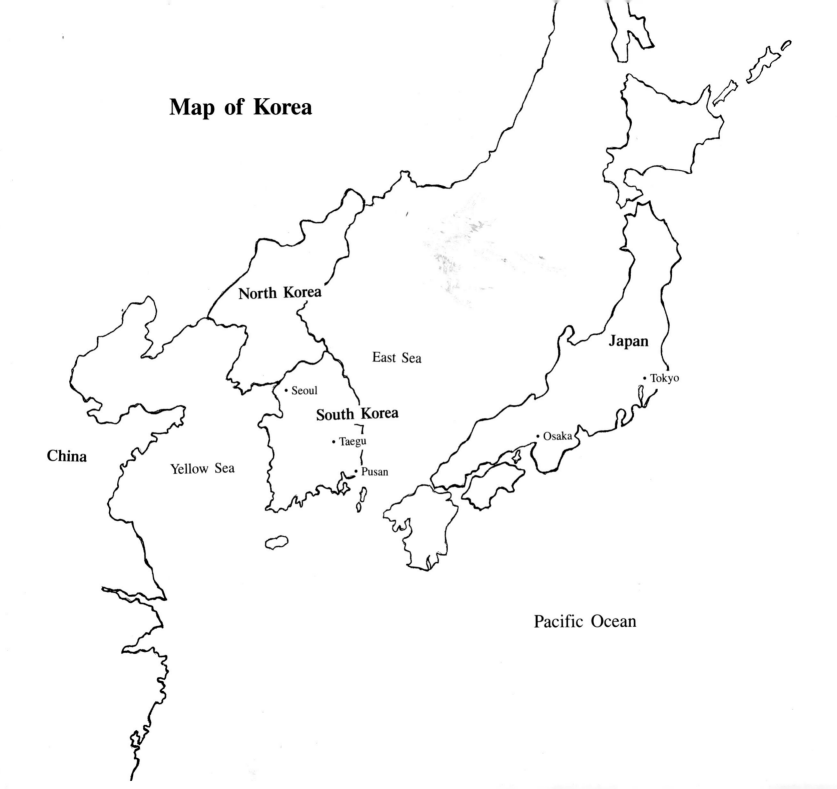

Map of Korea

China

North Korea

East Sea

Seoul

South Korea

Taegu

Pusan

Yellow Sea

Japan

Tokyo

Osaka

Pacific Ocean

FORWARD

In Korea, as in the United States, there are two kinds of holidays. One kind is the traditional, family-oriented, cultural or religious holiday, and the other is the political or historical holiday. Customs of holiday celebrations often change as times change. People and governments can create new holidays or stop celebrating old ones. This book is about traditional folk and family-oriented holidays and festivals celebrated in South Korea, specifically those the author of this book remembers from her childhood.* It describes the way Korean families have celebrated for ages.

Korea has been an agricultural country for many centuries. And Korean farmers have always used the lunar calendar, but during the twentieth century, the Government began to use the Gregorian calendar. As a result, today two kinds of calendars are used in South Korea. While the government officially uses the Gregorian calendar, the people have always celebrated their folk holidays according to the dates of the lunar calendar.** The lunar calendar is based on the cycles of the moon. This means each month begins close to a new moon, and the full moon appears around the middle of the month. Thus the life of the farmers has been closely tied to the cycles of the moon. Naturally, the moon—particularly the full moon—has been the focus of their holiday celebrations. In the full moon, they have found their greatest wonder, joy, beauty and even inspiration for poetry writing. They even believed that the full moon of the first lunar month was a source of information about weather for the coming year. This tradition of the full-moon celebrations is deeply felt by the people and still very much alive in the countryside.

So let us learn about traditional Korean holidays and festivals, and how they were, and still are, celebrated—with special activities, games, food and dress. These holidays can surely tell us a great deal about ancient Korean culture and customs.

* This book does not necessarily include all the holidays and festivals celebrated in South Korea.
** The time difference between the lunar and Gregorian (Western) calendars is about one month. The dates on the lunar calendar come approximately one month later than on the Gregorian calendar.

New Year's Obeisance

January/February

SŎL-NAL

Lunar New Year's Day

Lunar New Year's Day is the first day of the first month on the lunar calendar. It usually falls sometime between late January and late February on the Gregorian (Western) calendar.

For centuries, Koreans have celebrated this day as their traditional New Year's Day, although many Koreans today also celebrate New Year's Day on January 1. Only recently, the Korean government has made Lunar New Year's Day an official three-day holiday and named it Sŏl-Nal. Since it is the most important holiday to most Koreans, families make great preparations. They clean the house and try to pay off debts. They shop for gifts, prepare festive food and make new sets of traditional costumes (*han-bok*) for their children. The costumes are often made of brightly colored silk brocade. Girls receive a short blouse and long flowing skirt, and boys a loose jacket, often with a vest, and trousers.

It is a time for everyone to rejoice and hope for blessings in the New Year. On New Year's morning, children are expected to behave well and to be cheerful. They receive their New Year's costumes, including a pair of shoes and stockings. When they are dressed up in their new outfits, they make a formal bow (*se-bae*) to their parents or grandparents. In return, they receive from the elders blessings for the New Year and gifts of money.

It is also a time for family gatherings. Members of an extended family gather in the house of the oldest member of the family to offer memorial ceremonies (*che-sa*) in honor of the spirits of their departed ancestors.* A large table is set up to make an altar, with a wooden box that contains tablets listing the names of departed ancestors. Candles and incense are placed on the table, along with a variety of festive food, such as rice, vegetables, fish, meat, fruits, pancakes, rice cakes and *ttŏk-kuk* (a special

---

* It is the Buddhist tradition to worship the spirits of one's departed ancestors.

Memorial Ceremonies

New Year's soup made of oblong slices of rice cake). Some of the foods are piled high in tiers on pedestal plates. The eldest member of the family lights the candles, burns incense, and spreads a mat in front of the table. Then the family members make deep bows, standing or sitting. In Korea, bowing is a way of greeting or showing respect.

Traditionally, after the ceremony, a spoonful of food from each dish is placed on a large plate. Then it is scattered along the hedge or other places in the courtyard of the house. This is a custom inspired by Shamanist beliefs.* Those who practiced this custom believed the food would pacify or chase away the flying spirits that might bring sickness or bad luck to the family. After the ceremony, the family members sit down to enjoy the festive food.

Visiting is also a traditional part of New Year's celebrations. Usually on the second or third day of the season, adults make courtesy calls on their relatives and friends to offer holiday greetings. Guests usually bring a gift, which can be a bottle of rice wine, or New Year's holiday cakes or fruits. It is customary to serve the guests a special New Year's soup called *ttŏk-kuk,* along with a choice of drink or food—such as rice cakes or cookies. *Ttŏk-kuk* is a kind of soup made of beef broth, with beef, oval slices of glutinous rice cake, seaweed (laver), eggs, and other ingredients. *Mandu-kuk* is similar to *ttŏk-kuk* but includes dumplings instead of rice cake.

Traditionally, popular holiday games for children are kite-flying, seesawing, top-spinning or kicking the shuttlecock. Kite-flying is popular with both girls and boys. Some cities hold a kite-flying contest. Boys spin their wooden tops with a whiplash in the yard or on the frozen lake or river.

* Shamanism is a belief system that all natural phenomena are possessed of spirits which can affect any aspect of the living and their environment.

Korean Seesawing

A popular sport for girls is jumping on a long plank, the so-called Korean seesawing. One girl stands on each end of the plank, which is balanced on a rolled straw mat or over a dirt mound. When one girl bounces on the plank, the other goes up high in the air and comes down hard on the board with her feet together. Everyone cheers when one girl is able to bounce the other up higher into the air. Legend has it that this sport was started by girls who wanted to see what was going on beyond the walls of their courtyard. It is a sport requiring daring spirit.

A popular indoor game enjoyed by families is *yut*. It is a game played with a scoreboard and four elongated wooden sticks, flat on one side and curved like a half moon on the other. The sticks are thrown up into the air or down on the floor like dice. The way they land on the floor determines how many moves the player is allowed to make on the scoreboard.

For adults, there is a card game called *hwato*, which mean "flower cards." Adults of all ages enjoy this game, and so do children. The game is played with 48 small rectangular cards which have brightly colored illustrations of flowers, leaves, moon, sky and other objects. Each suit is made up of four cards that picture the same basic object. Two of the four cards in each suit have exactly the same picture and have no point value in themselves, but can be used to obtain cards of point value. The other two cards have an additional object in the basic pattern and have a certain point value in themselves. Many different games are played with *hwato*.

In the past, New Year's celebrations lasted for days, until *Tae-Bo-Rum*, the first full-moon festival.

Kite Flying

Yut Game

Great Moon Festival

February/March

TAE-BO-RŬM

Great Moon Festival

Tae-Bo-Rum, the first full moon, is celebrated on the 15th day of the first lunar month. It usually falls sometime between early February and early March on the Gregorian (Western) calendar. In the past this festival marked the end of the New Year's holiday season.

Traditionally, the full moon has been the focus of holiday celebrations because of its beauty and wonder. Particularly the first full moon of the New Year held a special meaning for the farmers, as they believed its color foretold the weather in the coming months. If the color of the first full moon was too pale, they believed there would be excessive rain. If too reddish, it meant there would be too little rain. But a golden moon meant perfect weather for their crops. Moreover, they believed that catching a view of the rising moon would bring them good luck in the coming year. So everyone eagerly wanted to catch a view of the rising moon.

From the early afternoon on, children would go up to hills in their village and, in the open space away from the wooded areas, they build a few small make-believe huts with twigs. Then they anxiously await the rise of the full moon from over the crest of a hill or over the horizon of the sea. As soon as they see the rim of the rising moon, they set fire to the huts and shout with joy, to signal the rise of the moon. The huts burn with flickering blazes of crackling fires, which send columns of smoke into the sky. The shouts of children echo across the village and bring the villagers up to the hills for a view of the rising moon. It is a time for joy and fun, especially for the children.

On this day Koreans crack and eat peanuts, walnuts or chestnuts, in the belief that they will not have pimples in the coming year. A special festive dish called *o-gok-pap* (five grain dish) is prepared for this festival. It is made of glutinous rice, black French beans, red beans, pine nuts, and a kind of millet. Vegetable side dishes are made of dried giant white radish, zucchini or squash, or edible bracken. Festive foods are often shared with friends and neighbors.

Cherry Blossom Festival

April

CHERRY BLOSSOM

FESTIVAL

In South Korea cherry trees bloom during the first two weeks of April. At this time the Cherry Blossom Festival is held in the southeastern seaside town of Chinhae, where the headquarters of the Korean Navy is now located.* This festival originated during the Japanese colonial period (1910-1945). After establishing Chinhae as their naval base, the Japanese planted a large number of cherry trees along the avenues of the town. During the season of cherry blossoms, the town came alive with thick clouds of pink and white blossoms. Families in the neighboring cities packed a lunch of *kim-pap* (rolled-rice wrapped in dried-laver sheets) and took their children to Chinhae on a day's excursion for a view of the cherry blossoms. And they had a picnic in the park under the clouds of cherry blossoms.

However, after the end of World War II, when Korea regained its independence from Japan, most of the cherry trees were uprooted from the town, perhaps because the people did not want to be reminded of Japanese oppression. Since then, new cherry trees have been planted in the town, and the legacy of the festival continues today but in a slightly different manner. Today families from the far corners of South Korea flock to Chinhae for a view of the cherry blossoms. As part of its celebration, the town stages a parade, traditional folk games and musical performances. It also holds ceremonies to celebrate the naval victories won by the famous Admiral Yi, who successfully defeated the invading Japanese naval forces in the mid-sixteenth century.

* Chinhae is located directly west of Pusan.

Buddha's Birthday

April/May

BUDDHA'S BIRTHDAY

Buddha's Birthday is observed on the eighth day of the fourth lunar month to honor the founder of Buddhism. It usually falls sometime between late April and late May on the Gregorian (Western) calendar. In 1975, Buddha's Birthday was made an official holiday in South Korea.

The religion of Buddhism has been in Korea for many centuries. During the era of the three Kingdoms, Paekje, Silla, Koryo (108 B.C.-1392 A.D.), each Kingdom adopted Buddhism as its state religion. Then, with the rise of the Choson dynasty at the end of 14th century, Buddhism began to lose its power as a political and social force to Confucianism. Although Korea has had many different religions throughout its history, Buddhism probably has had the greatest influence on the spiritual development and creativity of the Korean people. Many national historical and cultural treasures—the temples and pagodas and statues of Buddha that we see today— were directly inspired by Buddhism. Today in South Korea more people believe in Buddhism than in any other single religion.

On this day, in honor of Buddha's birth, many religious ceremonies and festive events are held at countless temples across the country. Temple courts are decorated with paper lanterns and paper flowers, often lotus, of various colors and shapes. Some believers make their own lanterns and hang them up in the temple courts of their choice. During the day many believers, dressed in their best clothes, flock to temples to offer their prayers. They may place flowers or burn incense on the altar in front of Buddha's image or statue. Then, standing up before the statue of Buddha, they pray fervently, clasping their hands, for Buddha's blessings.

At night the paraders march through the streets of many cities and towns, carrying candle-lighted lanterns. The candlelight symbolizes lighting the dark world and offering hope to the suffering or despaired.

Children's Day

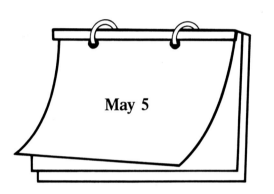

May 5

In 1975, the government of South Korea set May 5 as Children's Day, replacing the former "Boy's Day," which originated during the Japanese colonial period. The establishment of Children's Day acknowledges the importance of children, regardless of sex. At gatherings children sing a special song dedicated to Children's Day.

Children's Day is celebrated throughout the country with parades and special events. There are pageants and martial art demonstrations. Children are often dressed up in their traditional costumes and are treated to special entertainments, such as movies, museums, public zoos or amusement parks.

CHILDREN'S DAY

"Swing Day"

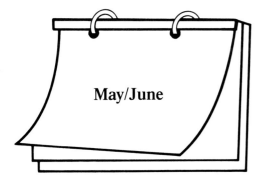

May/June

TAN-O DAY

"Swing Day"

Tan-O Day, also known as "swing day," is a centuries-old spring festival. It is celebrated on the fifth day of the fifth lunar month. It usually falls sometime between late May and late June on the Gregorian (Western) calendar.

On this day, girls wash their hair in iris water in the belief that it will make their hair shinier, softer, and even darker in color. Today, in rural areas, villagers prepare festive food and hold merry-making community events. Swing contests are held for women and girls. Usually a tall swing is tied onto the strong branch of an old tree, often oak, which stands upon a hill. For the occasion, the women are dressed up in their best traditional costumes and swing, always standing up, to compete in contests. The winner is the one who can swing higher in the sky more times than her competitors. Wrestling matches are held for boys, and often a bull is given to the winner as a prize. In some regions, mask dance-dramas are performed to expel evil spirits. In the cities, parents take their children out to parks, zoos or cultural centers to celebrate the day.

Graveside Visiting

September/October

CH'U-SŎK

Harvest Moon Festival

Harvest Moon Festival is celebrated on the 15th of the eighth lunar month, when the full moon is at its brightest. It usually falls sometime between early September and early October on the Gregorian (Western) calendar. A two-day official holiday, it is one of the two most celebrated holidays in South Korea, second only to Lunar New Year's Day.

This festival comes around the time when farmers harvest their new crops of rice, other grains and fruits. Family members, wherever they may be, return to their ancestral homes or gather at the house of the head of the family. In a sense, it is the Korean equivalent of America's Thanksgiving Day. Every child can expect a new set of traditional or modern clothes. It is a happy time for all Koreans.

In the morning families offer memorial ceremonies, as they do on Lunar New Year's Day, in honor of the spirits of their departed ancestors. They set up an altar on a large table with festive food, along with incense and candlelights. Family members make deep bows in front of the altar. After the ceremony, they sit down to festive food, which often includes fruits, vegetables, zucchini pancakes, meat, rice and wine. The special food prepared for this festival is the crescent-shaped rice cake, filled with honey-sweetened sesame seeds or red or mung bean paste. Later in the day families, all dressed up in their *chu-sok* clothes, visit their ancestral graveside to make offerings of food and thanksgiving bows.

During the holiday season city children are taken to amusement parks. Village girls are often dressed up in their traditional *chu-sok* costumes and may jump on the Korean seesaw. In the evening village children may play a tug-of-war game. However, viewing the full moon has always been the traditional way of celebrating for most Koreans. Those with a poetic spirit may write or read poetry in celebration of the full moon. Some Koreans believe that moon-viewing has greatly inspired the poetic spirit of the Korean people.

Winter Solstice Day

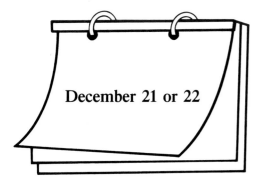

December 21 or 22

WINTER SOLSTICE DAY

Winter Solstice Day (*Tong-ji*) is the shortest day of the year. It is celebrated in Kyungsang-Nambo, the southeastern province of South Korea. Perhaps this celebration began because people needed a chance to cheer up a little, when daylight is in shortest supply. It's a festive custom that should be observed more widely in Korea.

It is a time for families to gather and enjoy a special food. Children look forward to this day because they can have red bean gruel with rice balls in it. In the past, as Winter Solstice Day approached, one used to hear the pounding of a mallet in a wooden mortar for making rice flour. Today most Koreans use machine-milled rice flour to make rice balls. Red bean gruel is made of soaked red beans. When the beans are cooked tender, they are mashed and run through a coarse strainer. The gruel is further cooked and seasoned with salt. Then rice balls are put in the bubbling gruel and cooked until they are tender.

Children are told that they must eat as many rice balls as the age they will become on the next New Year's Day.*

* Traditionally, in East Asia, one becomes one year older on New Year's Day, instead of on one's birthday.

Carolling

December 25

CHRISTMAS

Christmas is observed as an official holiday in South Korea. It is celebrated by Christians and their friends. In South Korea, Christians are growing fast in number. And Christmas is celebrated in much the same manner as in the United States. In big cities, department stores are attractively decorated with brightly colored lights and ornaments. Parents give gifts to their children. Many Koreans exchange Christmas cards with their friends and decorate their homes with artificial Christmas trees. Parties are given among friends and co-workers.

For Christians, a lot of holiday activities center around the church. These include Christmas Eve services, carol-singing, pageant-plays, gift-giving, and dinner parties. Of all the activities, early morning carol-singing is perhaps the most remarkable feature of the Christmas celebration. On Christmas Eve, some Christians gather in their church and pass the evening singing carols. From midnight until dawn, the carollers walk around the parts of town where other parish members reside, and sing carols standing in front of their houses. Often the family members come out to the gate to express their gratitude and may invite the carol-singers into their house for a midnight snack.

For most Koreans, however, Christmas is not the most celebrated holiday. Their most celebrated holidays are those traditional folk festivals—Lunar New Year's Day, Tan-O Day and Harvest Moon Festival Day.

About the Author

Frances M. Koh, nationally recognized author with her first book, *Oriental Children in American Homes,* is an editor and publisher. This is her fourth book, and she is at work on several other projects, including one on intercountry adoption. Her other pursuits include writing short stories and photography.

About the Illustrator

Liz B. Dodson, a professional artist, has illustrated many children's books for publishers in the United States and abroad.